RABBITS

Fiona Patchett

Designed by Jan McCafferty
Edited by Fiona Watt

Illustrations by Christyan Fox
Photographs by Jane Burton

CONTENTS

2   Different rabbits
4   Choosing a rabbit
6   What will I need?
8   Settling in
10 Outdoors
12 Feeding
14 Fresh food
16 Playing
18 Taming your rabbit
20 Fur
22 What does it mean?
24 Cleaning out
26 Staying healthy
28 Going to the vet
29 Going away
30 Indoor rabbits
32 Index

With additional photographs by Howard Allman
Consultant: John Hodgkiss
With thanks to Andrew Kirby

Different rabbits

Rabbits are gentle, friendly animals that make excellent pets. There are about fifty types, or breeds, of rabbits you can choose from. This book will help you to choose your first rabbit and show you how to look after it.

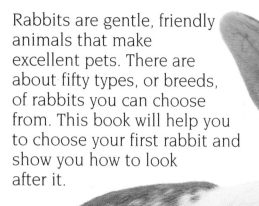

Size

Some types of rabbits grow very big, others stay small. When you buy a rabbit, ask how big it will grow. Get one you will be able to lift when it is fully-grown.

A large rabbit can eat ten times the amount of a small one.

Both these rabbits are fully-grown adults.

This is a Butterfly Pattern rabbit. This type of rabbit can weigh up to 9kg (4½ lbs).

This is called a Netherland Dwarf rabbit. It weighs 1kg (2¼ lbs). This is about the same as a bag of sugar.

Wild rabbits

Pet rabbits are related to the wild rabbits you see in the countryside. Some look a bit like wild rabbits and often behave in the same way. All rabbits belong to a family of animals which includes hares and animals called pikas. Hares and pikas only live in the wild. They are not kept as pets.

Hares are bigger than rabbits, with longer ears and stronger legs. They can run very fast.

Pikas are smaller than rabbits. They live in North America and Asia.

Types of fur

Different breeds of rabbits have different types and lengths of fur. They have different markings too. Some breeds, such as Angora rabbits, have very long fur. They need a lot of attention because their fur needs brushing every day.

Brown, speckled fur is called agouti. Wild rabbits have this type of fur. So do some pet rabbits.

Cross breeds

Two different breeds of rabbits will have babies which look like a mixture of both parents. These are called cross breeds.

Fur that is 2–3cm (1in) long is called normal fur. This Black Dutch rabbit has normal fur.

Angora rabbits have soft, fluffy fur, called wool.

Big ears

Some rabbits, called lop-eared rabbits, have big, droopy ears. Some breeds have ears that grow so big they touch the ground. Very big ears can get dirty and even make the rabbit trip.

This lop-eared rabbit has average-sized ears.

Choosing a rabbit

Baby rabbits are ready to leave their mother when they are nine weeks old. Try to buy a rabbit which is about this age. Young rabbits are easier to tame than adult ones.

These are some of the things you should look for when you choose a rabbit:

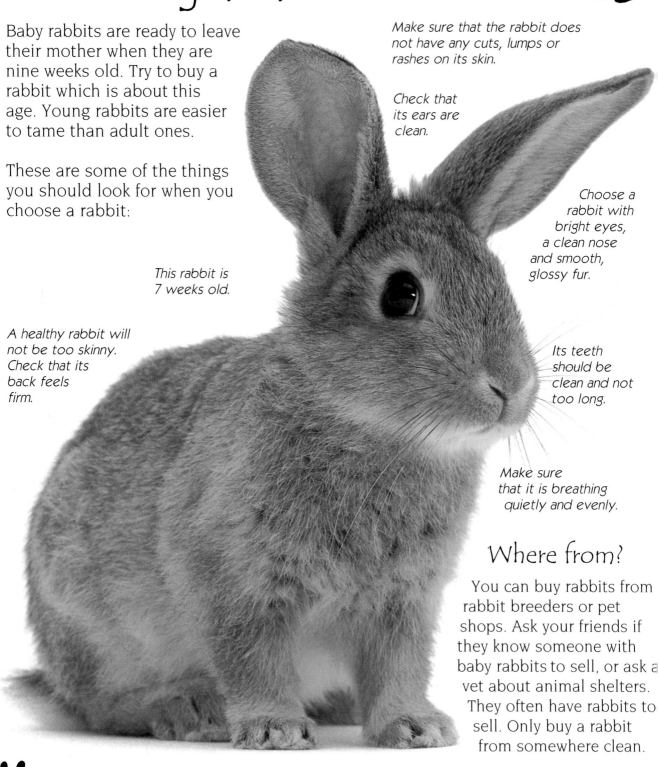

Make sure that the rabbit does not have any cuts, lumps or rashes on its skin.

Check that its ears are clean.

Choose a rabbit with bright eyes, a clean nose and smooth, glossy fur.

This rabbit is 7 weeks old.

A healthy rabbit will not be too skinny. Check that its back feels firm.

Its teeth should be clean and not too long.

Make sure that it is breathing quietly and evenly.

Where from?

You can buy rabbits from rabbit breeders or pet shops. Ask your friends if they know someone with baby rabbits to sell, or ask a vet about animal shelters. They often have rabbits to sell. Only buy a rabbit from somewhere clean.

Which one?

Watch all the rabbits for a little while. Choose the one that looks the most lively and playful.

Ask the owner to show you how to pick it up. Check that it is healthy. Stroke it and decide if you like it.

Ask if the rabbit is a male or a female. Male rabbits are called bucks and females are called does.

Buying two rabbits

Two sisters get along best.

Wild rabbits live together in large groups. Pet rabbits can also live with another rabbit (see pages 8-9). If you buy two, try to get them from the same family. Females get along well. Two males together may fight. If a male and a female rabbit live together, they will have babies unless the male rabbit has an operation.

What will I need?

Before you bring your rabbit home, make sure you are prepared. You can buy all the things you will need from a good pet shop.

Carrying box

When you buy a rabbit, you will need a box so you can carry it home. You can buy carrying boxes from pet shops or you could use a strong cardboard box. Get someone to help you make air holes in the cardboard.

Food and drink

Heavy pottery dishes are good as they do not tip over.

You will need to buy a food dish for your rabbit and some rabbit food (see pages 12-15).

Line the carrying box with hay.

Hay rack

Ask in a pet shop for rabbit hay. Your rabbit can eat hay from the floor of its hutch or from a rack.

Turn the bottle upside down.

Attach the water bottle to the hutch.

Bring your rabbit home as quickly as possible.

Water bottles keep your rabbit's water clean. Buy one with a metal spout so your rabbit can't chew it.

Hutches

Most pet rabbits live in hutches. Hutches are divided in two - a living area, where the rabbit eats, and a warm, safe area where it can hide away and sleep. You can leave a hutch outside all year, as long as it is in a sheltered spot, away from strong sunlight and winds.

The solid door keeps the rabbit warm while it sleeps.

The wire door lets fresh air into the living area.

A hutch should be at least 90cm (3ft) long and high enough for your rabbit to stand upright.

It's a good idea to get a hutch with legs to keep it off damp ground.

Make sure the hutch roof is waterproof too.

Bedding

1. Put a layer of paper on the floor of the hutch. Cover it with wood shavings. In the sleeping area, you can also put down hay for your rabbit to make its bed from.

2. Rabbits are tidy animals and tend to leave their droppings in one corner of their hutch. Watch where that is and put some extra wood shavings in that corner.

Settling in

When you bring your rabbit home, it may be very frightened. It will take a few days to settle in and get to know you. Rabbits can share a hutch with another rabbit or a guinea pig. Get them at the same time, so that neither one makes the hutch their home before the other one moves in.

First steps

Don't stand up with your rabbit or it may jump and hurt itself.

1. When you get your rabbit home, put the carrying box near the hutch. Open the box and stroke your rabbit.

2. Sit down so your rabbit is facing you. To lift it up, put one hand across its neck and the other under its bottom.

3. Carefully lift your rabbit. Use one hand to support its bottom and the other to hold its head against your chest.

Stroke your rabbit gently.

Always stroke it in the direction that its fur grows.

4. Leave your rabbit for two days to settle into its hutch. Feed it, but don't pick it up during this time.

Two pets

You should introduce two pets when they are both young. Put the smaller one into the hutch first. Leave the other in a carrying box near the front of the hutch. Your pets will get used to the smell of each other. After a few hours put the bigger pet into the hutch.

Rabbits and guinea pigs get along well.

Making friends

Speak quietly to your rabbit.

Before you start playing with your rabbit, it will need to get used to you. Start by giving it some food, such as a small piece of carrot, from your hand.

When your rabbit is used to you feeding it, then start to stroke it gently. When it is happy with you stroking it, then you can lift it out of its hutch.

Outdoors

Wild rabbits can eat fresh grass whenever they want. If you can, let your rabbit out of its hutch to eat grass, or graze, for as long as possible every day. You should let it eat grass somewhere safe where it will not be able to escape.

Runs and grazing arks

Runs and grazing arks are safe places, made from wood and wire mesh, where rabbits can eat grass. You attach a run to the front of a hutch so your rabbit can get shelter from the heat and the rain. Grazing arks are not attached to hutches. The best kinds have a solid roof at one end to provide shelter.

A grazing ark should be high enough so your rabbit can stand upright on its back legs.

Put hay in the sheltered area so your rabbit can sleep there if it wants.

Put your rabbit's food dish into the ark.

This is a grazing ark. It is made from wood and wire mesh.

An ark should be at least 2m (6ft) long and 1m (3ft) wide.

Attach a water bottle to the wire mesh.

The wire mesh keeps wild animals out and stops your rabbit from escaping.

Wire mesh on the floor of a run or a grazing ark stops your rabbit from burrowing out (see page 17). Make sure this mesh is wide enough to let grass grow through. If you let your rabbit graze in one spot for too long, it will eat all the grass. An ark can be moved to a new patch of grass each day.

A safe spot

Put the run or grazing ark where there is lots of healthy grass. Weedkiller on the grass and some plants, such as daisies and buttercups, can poison rabbits.

Rabbits do not like to be too hot or too cold. Put the grazing ark in a place that is sheltered from strong winds, rain and bright sunlight.

Setting up the ark

At night

Put hay in the sheltered area.

1. Although your rabbit will have plenty of fresh grass to eat, it will need a supply of dried food, hay and water in its ark too.

2. Lift your rabbit out of its hutch and put it into the ark. Close the door and fasten it so your rabbit can't escape.

Put your rabbit into its hutch at night. Move the ark onto a new patch of fresh grass for the next day.

Feeding

Rabbits need a variety of dried food and fresh food (see pages 14-15). They like to eat at the same time each day. It is best to feed them dried food in the morning and fresh food in the evening. Start off feeding your rabbit exactly the same food it ate before you bought it.

Rabbit pellets

Dried food

Dried food mixture contains dried fruits, vegetables and seeds. Twice a week, you can feed your rabbit pellets as well as mixture. Pellets contain extra things to make your rabbit healthy.

There are lots of different dried fruits and vegetables in this mixture, such as carrots, bananas and peas.

How much?

Small rabbits eat about two tablespoons of mixture. Big rabbits can eat half a dishful.

Leave the food in the hutch all day.

When your rabbit is young, put plenty of food in its dish every morning. It will eat as much as it needs.

Your rabbit will eat more as it gets older. If it eats all the food in the dish, give it more the next day.

Make sure your rabbit eats everything in the mixture. If it leaves anything, give it less the next day.

Water

Rabbits need lots of water and must be able to drink it at all times, especially when the weather is hot. Fill your rabbit's bottle with fresh water every day.

Attach the water bottle to the side of the hutch so your rabbit can reach it.

Hay

Hay is dried grass. Rabbits like to munch hay on and off all day, so make sure there is always plenty in your rabbit's hutch.

Salt Block

You can buy salt blocks from pet shops.

Some rabbit food contains salt, but your rabbit may need to eat more. Ask for advice in a pet shop.

Rabbits can stand up on their back legs to reach the spout of the water bottle.

Fresh food

Your rabbit will need to eat a little fresh food, such as fruit and vegetables, every day, as well as dried food. After a few weeks, you should slowly introduce your rabbit to some new types of food.

What fresh food to give

Rabbits like hard fruit and raw vegetables, like apples, pears and raw carrots. Some rabbits like soft food, such as lettuce and tomato, but do not feed these too often. Soft food can make your rabbit ill. Always start by giving your rabbit a small amount first to find out if it likes it.

Cauliflower

Lettuce

Tomato

Peas

Cucumber

Parsnip

Celery

A carrot and a small piece of apple would be the right daily amount for a small rabbit.

Two sticks of celery and half a pear would be the right daily amount for a large rabbit.

Treats

You can give your rabbit treats, but not too often. Your rabbit may like a strawberry or a raspberry. Try giving your rabbit different fruit and vegetables to find out what it likes.

Preparing fresh food

Put fresh food in your rabbit's dish late in the afternoon or early in the evening.

1. Wash the fruit and vegetables to get rid of any chemicals. Carefully cut it into chunky pieces.

2. Remove any left over dried food. Wash the dish and put in several pieces of fresh food.

3. Before bed, take away any uneaten food. Food that starts to go bad can make your rabbit very ill.

New food

When you give your rabbit something it hasn't tried before, give a small amount first. If it finishes the food and does not get ill, you can give it that food again. If it doesn't eat much, it probably doesn't like it.

Give your rabbit one or two small pieces of any new food at first.

Playing

Rabbits like playing and need lots of exercise. Let your rabbit out of its hutch at least once a day. Rabbits are most active in the morning and evening so these are the best times. Let your rabbit play in a run or grazing ark (see page 10) or in any enclosed place where it cannot escape.

Rabbits like hiding in flower pots.

Adventure playground

You can make an adventure playground for your rabbit by putting out interesting things, such as flower pots, pieces of drainpipe and stones, for it to discover and play with.

Rabbits will crawl through short drainpipes.

Put out pebbles for your rabbit to explore.

Make sure the pipes are wide enough for your rabbit to fit through.

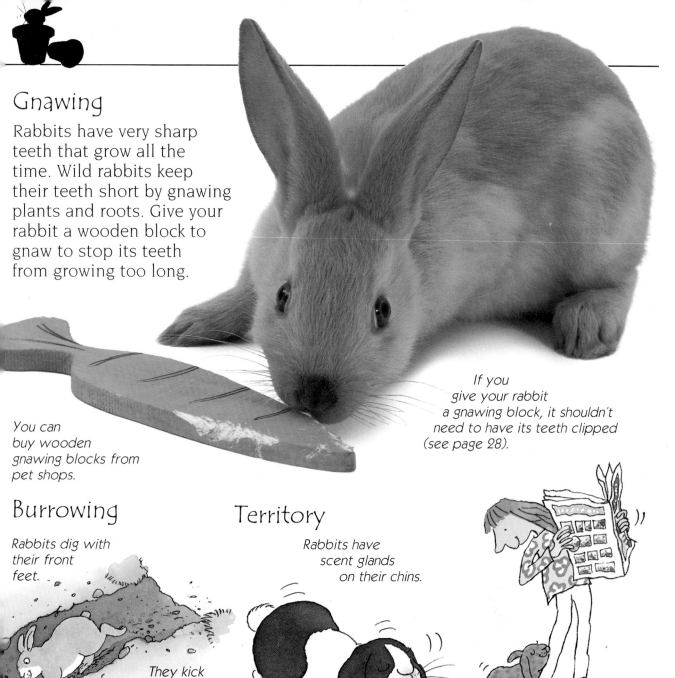

Gnawing

Rabbits have very sharp teeth that grow all the time. Wild rabbits keep their teeth short by gnawing plants and roots. Give your rabbit a wooden block to gnaw to stop its teeth from growing too long.

You can buy wooden gnawing blocks from pet shops.

If you give your rabbit a gnawing block, it shouldn't need to have its teeth clipped (see page 28).

Burrowing

Rabbits dig with their front feet.

They kick the soil out of the way with their back feet.

Wild rabbits burrow tunnels underground to live in. Your pet rabbit may also try to burrow when it is playing.

Territory

Rabbits have scent glands on their chins.

Rabbits mark the area where they feel safe with a scent that they can smell, but humans can't. This area is their territory.

Your rabbit may try to rub its scent on its play things. If its rubs its scent on you and any other pets, it is just being friendly.

Taming your rabbit

The more you handle your rabbit, the tamer it will become. Stroke it every day, especially if it lives in a hutch on its own. Rabbits often run away, burrow or gnaw things when you don't want them to. If your rabbit is tame, you will be able to train it to do what you want more easily.

Handling tips

When you pick up your rabbit (see page 8), do not walk around with it. It may jump out of your arms and hurt itself. Sit and stroke it, but not for too long.

Stroke your rabbit gently to keep it calm.

Rabbits are strong and will kick you if they are not happy. If your rabbit struggles, put it back into its hutch or grazing ark.

Put your rabbit's back legs down first, so if it kicks it won't hurt you.

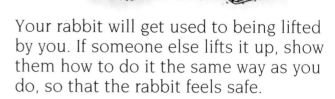

Your rabbit will get used to being lifted by you. If someone else lifts it up, show them how to do it the same way as you do, so that the rabbit feels safe.

Training

You should start teaching your rabbit what it can and can't do from an early age. Rabbits learn much quicker when they are young.

Reward your rabbit with a treat, such as a piece of carrot.

1. If your rabbit does something naughty, point at it, say its name and 'No!' in a firm voice.

2. When your rabbit stops being naughty, reward it by stroking it and giving it some food as a treat.

Runaway rabbits

1. When your rabbit is out playing, it may be difficult to catch. Do not chase it as this will frighten it.

2. Hold some food in your hand, near your rabbit. This will tempt it to come to you.

3. Let your rabbit eat the food. Pick up your rabbit. Carry it back to its hutch or to a grazing ark.

Fur

Fur is very important because it keeps your rabbit warm. Rabbit fur is slightly oily to make it waterproof. Rabbits clean their own fur, but you can help by grooming it too.

It uses its tongue like a face-cloth . . .

Keeping clean

Rabbits spend a lot of time washing and grooming. They use their teeth, tongue and paws to pick out any dirt that is stuck in their fur.

. . . and is using its claws like a comb to clean its fur.

Rabbits clean all parts of their body. This rabbit is cleaning its feet.

The rabbit is holding its ear as it cleans the end of it.

It twists around to clean all its fur.

Grooming

If you groom your rabbit once a week, its fur should stay clean and healthy. Rabbits groom each other as a way of making friends. This is also a good way for your rabbit to get used to you.

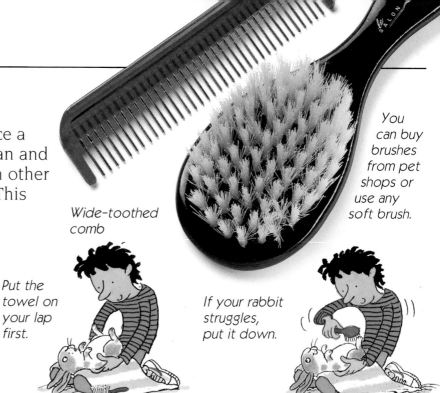

Wide-toothed comb

You can buy brushes from pet shops or use any soft brush.

Put the towel on your lap first.

If your rabbit struggles, put it down.

1. Sit your rabbit on an old towel. Brush the fur on its back, from its neck moving towards its tail.

2. Lift your rabbit onto your lap, so its stomach is facing you and its head is close to your knees.

3. Gently brush your rabbit's stomach, moving the brush in the direction that the fur grows.

Shedding

Once or twice a year, your rabbit may shed more fur than usual. When this happens, groom it every day to get rid of loose fur.

Long-haired rabbits

Rabbits with long fur need to be groomed every day. Brush the fur, one section at a time, from the roots to the ends. Then, do the same with a comb.

Hold each section of fur as you brush or comb it.

What does it mean?

Rabbits let each other know how they feel by their different movements. If you watch your rabbit closely, you can learn to understand what mood it is in.

On the lookout

When rabbits see or hear something strange, they stand up on their back legs so they can have a better look. Their ears stand up straight so they can hear every sound. Your rabbit may stand like this if it feels in danger or if it sees you bringing it some food.

This rabbit's ears are standing upright so it can listen for danger.

Its eyes are in the sides of its head. This lets it see in front and behind.

Feeling scared

In the wild, when rabbits are scared, they usually run away. Their tails are white underneath so that when they run, it signals danger to other rabbits.

This rabbit is trying not to be seen.

If a rabbit is very scared, it will lie still, close to the ground and fold its ears back, hoping not to be seen. If your rabbit does this, leave it alone or you may frighten it more.

22

Something new

Rabbits have a very good sense of smell. If they see something new, they sniff it to get used to the new smell. They use their whiskers to feel if it is safe, too.

Rabbits sniff each other when they meet.

Bathtime

You may see your rabbit flick one of its paws out in front of it. This means it is probably going to start grooming itself.

If your rabbit flicks its paw, leave it to groom alone.

Eating droppings

Don't worry if you see your rabbit eat some of its droppings. Rabbits do this so they can digest their food twice.

No threats

Rabbits sometimes sunbathe like this too.

If you see your rabbit stretched out on its tummy, like this, it is relaxed and feels safe. If your rabbit wants to go to sleep, it will shut its eyes and lie on one side with one leg stretched out. Do not disturb your rabbit when it is asleep.

Cleaning out

Rabbits are very tidy animals, but you should clean your rabbit's hutch regularly or it could get ill. While you clean its hutch, lift your rabbit into a grazing ark or a carrying box. Always wash your hands well when you have finished cleaning out, to get rid of any germs.

Every day

Make sure your rabbit has fresh hay to eat. If it has a hay rack, you can use the old hay from the rack as new bedding.

Your rabbit will rub its scent on its new bedding.

After you have cleaned the hutch your rabbit may rearrange the hay you have put in.

Rabbits usually leave their droppings in a pile in a corner of their living area. You can remove these with a spatula or a plastic spade.

Throw away any old food from your rabbit's dish. Wash it well and dry it with an old towel.

Once or twice a week

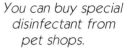

Scrape the dirt from the corners with a spatula.

You can buy special disinfectant from pet shops.

1. Throw away the hay, wood shavings and paper. Use a dustpan and brush to sweep out the hutch.

2. Dip a brush into some warm, soapy water. Scrub the inside of the hutch. Rinse it with clean water.

3. Let the hutch dry. Spray it with disinfectant. Lay paper in the bottom. Cover it with wood shavings and hay.

Wash and dry the hay rack.

These are the things you need. Don't use them to clean anything else but your rabbit's hutch.

Disinfectant

Dustpan and brush

Bucket and a drying cloth

4. Push a brush into the water bottle. Scrub inside it with soapy water, then rinse it. Wash your hands when you have finished.

Dishwashing liquid

Spatula

Bottle brush

Scrubbing brush

Staying healthy

If you look after your rabbit properly, it should stay healthy. Check your rabbit every day to make sure that it is well. If you think your rabbit is ill, look in your telephone directory for the number of a local vet. Ask for advice first before taking your rabbit there. Visiting the vet can be expensive.

Fleas and lice

If you see your rabbit scratching a lot, it may have fleas or lice. These are little creatures that live in rabbit fur and make its skin itch. Fleas are dark and shiny and lice look like salt.

Fleas and lice can make your rabbit very uncomfortable.

Follow the instructions carefully for using the powder.

If you think your rabbit has fleas or lice, put on some old gloves, lift your rabbit into a carrying box and clean its hutch.

You can buy special powder from pet shops to get rid of the fleas or lice on your rabbit's fur.

Health checks

Phone a vet for advice if you think your rabbit is ill.

Your rabbit may be ill if it has trouble breathing, or if it is not eating or drinking much.

Check that your rabbit's eyes, nose and ears are not runny. If they are, it may have a cold.

If your rabbit is wounded, wash the wound with warm water mixed with a little antiseptic.

Looking after your rabbit

Let your rabbit rest in a warm, quiet place.

If your rabbit looks ill, clean its hutch to get rid of any germs. Give your rabbit lots of water to drink and cover its hutch to keep it warm.

Getting older

This rabbit is nine years old.

Most rabbits live to be six to eight years old. As your rabbit gets older, it will sleep a lot more and will need more help keeping clean.

Going to the vet

When you get a rabbit, you may have to take it to a vet for some injections. If you check your rabbit's health at home, you will only need to take it to a vet if it looks very ill, or its teeth or claws get too long. If you want to keep a male and a female rabbit together, the male will need an operation called neutering. You should ask your vet about this when you first take it.

A vet clipping a rabbit's claws

Getting there

Take your rabbit to the vet in its carrying box. Keep it as still and quiet on the journey as possible. Cover the box with a cloth so your rabbit won't get scared by other animals waiting to see the vet.

Teeth and claws

Your rabbit's claws should be ½cm (¼in) from its skin.

Your rabbit's teeth should be straight with the top teeth overlapping the lower ones.

Your rabbit's claws may grow too long. If they do, take it to a vet or a pet shop to have them clipped.

If your rabbit's teeth grow too long it will not be able to eat. You will need to ask a vet to cut them.

Injections

Your rabbit may need to have some injections to stop it from getting some nasty diseases.

Going away

You can go away overnight as long as you make sure your rabbit has enough water, hay and food in its hutch. If you go away for longer, you must find someone to look after your rabbit. Try to find someone who knows about rabbits.

Before you go

Make a list of everything that needs to be done. Your rabbit should be fed the same amount of food and let out to exercise at the same time as usual.

Take your rabbit to a friend's house in a carrying box.

This carrying box is made from wicker. Some are made from plastic or cardboard (see page 6).

If you are away for longer than a week, the hutch will need to be cleaned and your rabbit will need to be groomed as well. Remember to leave enough equipment.

Take all the things your rabbit will need.

If your friend lives too far away to visit your rabbit every day, you will need to take your rabbit there. Take your rabbit's food, bedding and equipment too. Take its hutch, but clean it out first.

Indoor rabbits

You can keep a pet rabbit indoors, as long as it gets plenty of exercise. Make sure your house is safe for your rabbit.

Remember that rabbits like gnawing and scratching, so take away anything your rabbit might damage.

Fill the wooden box with hay.

Put wood shavings in the bottom.

Tape electric wires so your rabbit can't reach them.

Close any doors before you let your rabbit out.

Put the dishes on sheets of paper.

1. An indoor rabbit will need a cage to live in. Put a wooden box inside for it to sleep in.

2. Keep your rabbit away from dangers such as people's feet, hot drinks and anything sharp.

3. Put food, water and hay in the cage. Put food and water in dishes outside the cage too.

When your rabbit is out playing, always keep an eye on it, so it doesn't escape or get hurt.

Rabbits like to explore cushions.

Toilet training

If you keep your rabbit indoors, you should train it to go to the toilet in one place. Rabbits are clean animals and usually go to the toilet in the same place. Watch where that is and put a plastic tray down there. Your rabbit will soon learn to go there by itself. You can buy special trays, called litter trays, from pet shops.

Fill the litter tray with wood shavings or cat litter.

Empty your rabbit's litter tray every day. Wash it with warm water and disinfectant every week.

Put the tray on a piece of newspaper.

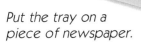

If your rabbit goes to the toilet outside the tray, wipe a little vinegar on that spot. Rabbits dislike the smell so much, they learn not to go there again.

INDEX

bedding, 7, 24, 30
breathing, 4, 27
breeds, 2-3
brushing your rabbit, 21
burrowing, 10, 17

cages, 30
carrying box, 6, 8, 9, 29
cat litter, 31
claws, 20, 28
cleaning out, 24-25
cross breeds, 3

droppings, 7, 23, 24

ears, 4, 22
eyes, 4, 22

feeding, 6, 8, 9, 10, 11,
  12-13, 14-15, 19, 30
fleas, 26
food,
  dish, 6, 12, 15, 24, 30
  dried, 12
  fresh, 14-15
  pellets, 12
fur, 3, 20-21

gnawing, 17, 30
gnawing blocks, 17
grazing, 10-11
grazing ark, 10-11, 16
grooming, 20-21, 23
guinea pigs, 8, 9

handling your rabbit, 18
hares, 2
hay, 6, 7, 10, 11, 13, 24, 30
healthy rabbits, 4, 26-27
hutches, 7, 8, 25

indoor rabbits, 30-31
injections, 28

lice, 26
litter trays, 31
long-haired rabbits, 3, 21
lop-eared rabbits, 3

neutering, 28

older rabbits, 27

picking up your rabbit, 8, 18

playing, 16-17
poisons, 11

runs, 10-11, 16

salt blocks, 13
scent, 17, 24
shedding fur, 21
sleeping, 7, 10, 23, 30
smell, 9, 17, 23
stroking, 8, 9, 18

taming, 4, 18-19
teeth, 4, 17, 20, 28
territory, 17
toilet training, 31
tongue, 20
training, 19
treats, 14, 19
two rabbits, 5, 8, 9

vets, 26, 28

water, 6, 13, 27, 30
wild rabbits, 2, 5, 10, 17
wood shavings, 7, 25, 30, 3
wounds, 27

With thanks to:
Kathryn Main, Peter Richards and the people who lent their pets.
Lifestyles UK Ltd, Upton Warren, Bromsgrove, Worcestershire, B61 7EY
The Hutch Company, Herne Bay, Kent, CT6 8JZ